For Carmela, the firefly that lights up my life. – KF

To Olivia, with love from your big sis. – ES

LCCN 2016961450
ISBN 9781943147328

Text copyright © 2017 by Kristin Foote
Illustrations by Erica Salcedo
Illustrations copyright © 2017 The Innovation Press

Published by The Innovation Press
1001 4th Avenue, Suite 3200, Seattle, WA 98154
www.theinnovationpress.com

Printed and bound by Worzalla
Production Date: May 2017
Plant Location: Stevens Point,
Wisconsin

Cover lettering by Nicole LaRue
Cover art by Erica Salcedo
Book layout by Tim Martyn

HOW to SURVIVE AS A FIREFLY

WRITTEN BY KRISTEN FOOTE ILLUSTRATED BY ERICA SALCEDO

Metamorphosis (noun)

1. The changes that some animals go through in how they look and act during the process of becoming adults

In other words, you can't be larvae forever! Fireflies go through a type of metamorphosis called **COMPLETE** metamorphosis. This means you don't just change once. You have four different life cycle stages from when you're an egg until you're an adult! It will be up to **YOU** to head back underground and finish the larva and pupa stages after our lessons today!

FUN FACT:
Bees, ants, mosquitoes, and butterflies also go through complete metamorphosis.

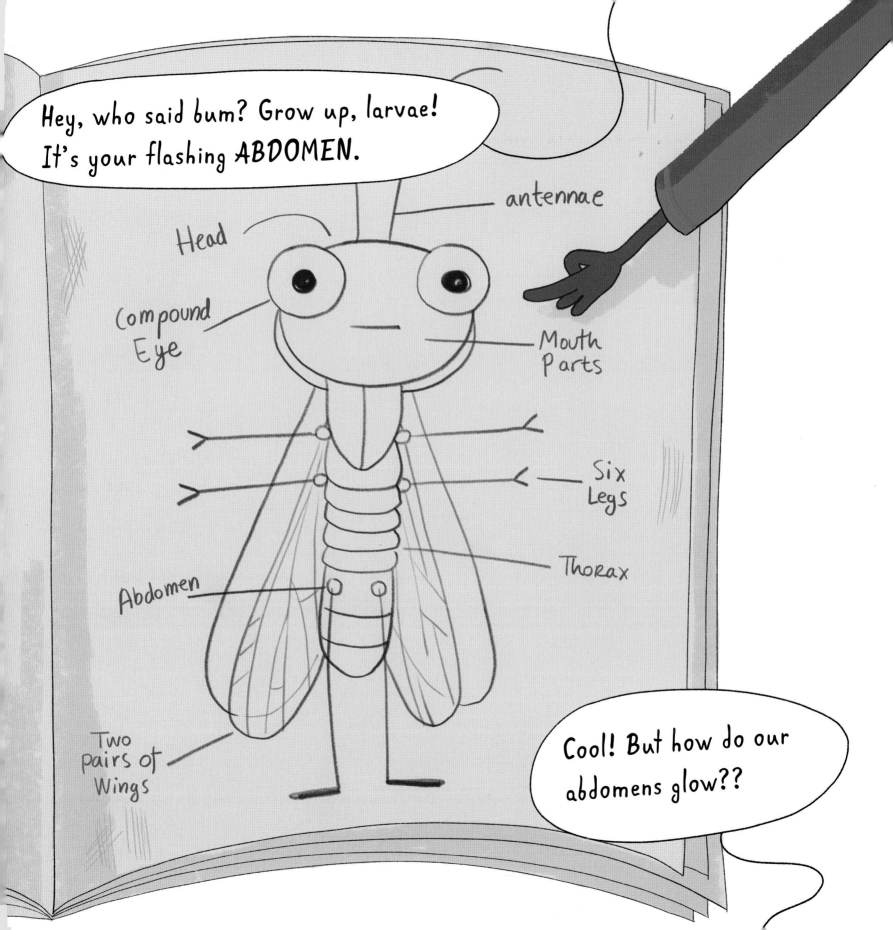

Got all that? Good! It's time for a pop quiz:
When you're an adult, after a long night's work, what's for dinner?

A) French Fried Worms
B) Snotty Snail Soup
C) Assorted Slug Salad
D) All of the above

TRICK QUESTION! None of the above. That's why you need
to be eating all the time, larvae! Adults don't have
time to eat. Now go catch a slug before we move
on to the last lesson.

FLORAL FACT:
Although many adult fireflies do not eat, scientists think some
species may eat flower nectar or pollen. *Photinus pyralis* adults
have also been known to drink water from leaves.

As an adult firefly, you have just one job. By the time you are grown up, you'll have only five to thirty days left to live. Do not bother eating or playing with friends. The **ONLY** thing you need to worry about is finding a mate so you can leave behind firefly eggs before you die. To do this, you have to find a firefly with a flashing pattern or glow that matches up with yours. And what's this glow called?

FLASHY FACT:
There are more than 2,000 species of fireflies. Not all of them glow, but each species that glows has a unique flashing pattern.

FINDING A MATE 101

Do skip the talking and goofing around. Time is ticking!

Do find a good place to search for a mate. Remember, dark areas with tall, damp grass or trees are where most fireflies hang out.

Do avoid giants with nets and jars. They look like they are having fun! But trust me, it's no fun for you.

Do locate your nearest escape route in case of an emergency (See Aggressive Mimicry Definition).

Don't get crazy with your flashes. This will confuse the other fireflies.

Don't get distracted or you will miss your mate's signal! Females — stay in one spot. Males — fly around and flash your pattern. The right mate for you will flash the matching pattern a few seconds after you, signaling you to go near her.

Don't go searching in places with lots of light. What may seem like the perfect match could be someone's flashlight, lantern, or worse . . . headlights! This is awkward (and messy) for everyone involved. Stick to dark areas with lots of tall grass or trees.

FATAL FACT:
Scientists think that *Photuris* fireflies eat *Photinus pyralis* fireflies because when *Photuris* swallow a certain chemical in the blood of a *Photinus pyralis*, it makes them taste bad to other predators.

For the males of the bunch, watch out for predators who want to eat you. And I'm not talking about the usual frogs, birds, and spiders. You need to beware of females from the firefly genus, *Photuris*! These tricky fireflies copy the *Photinus pyralis* female's flashing pattern to make you think they're the same species. Then they try to eat you! This is called Aggressive Mimicry. Keep searching until you find a mate who doesn't want you for dinner.

Aggressive Mimicry (noun)
1. When a predator changes how it looks or acts to trick you, so that it can eat you

MY FRIEND FREDDY TOLD ME WE ARE FLIES. BUT MY OTHER FRIEND JIMMY SAID WE ARE BUGS. WHO IS RIGHT?

Neither! I know some people call you fireflies and lightning bugs. Humans come up with the funniest names! The truth is you're not a fly OR a bug! Yes, you are an insect like flies and bugs, which means you have six legs and a head, thorax, and abdomen. But you are a different kind of insect. You are a winged beetle!

SOMETHING IS WRONG WITH MY BUM. IT DOESN'T LIGHT UP! HOW WILL I EVER FIND A MATE?

Well, first of all, it's not your bum that lights up. It's your abdomen! Second, just relax. Some species of fireflies don't glow as adults at all. It's OK! You must not be a *Photinus pyralis* firefly. You are a species that has chemicals in your body called pheromones. You can put those chemicals into the air and your true mate will come find you. Think of it as insect perfume!

I WAS MINDING MY OWN BUSINESS, BUT NOW I'M STUCK IN A JAR WITH GIANTS STARING AT ME AND SHAKING ME. WHAT SHOULD I DO?

Fly to the bottom of the jar and pretend to be dead. The giants might become bored with you and dump you out.

I AM HAVING A HARD TIME FINDING A MATE. I FEEL SO ALONE. WHAT SHOULD I DO?

Ask yourself these two questions:

1. Are you in Antarctica? If so, fire your travel agent immediately and end your vacation. It is the only continent where fireflies do not live. Of course you are shivering and alone! I hear the Great Smoky Mountains are nice this time of year.

2. Are you in a dark, damp area with lots of grass and trees? What do you mean, no? Have you not been paying attention? Go back and read your notes! NOW!

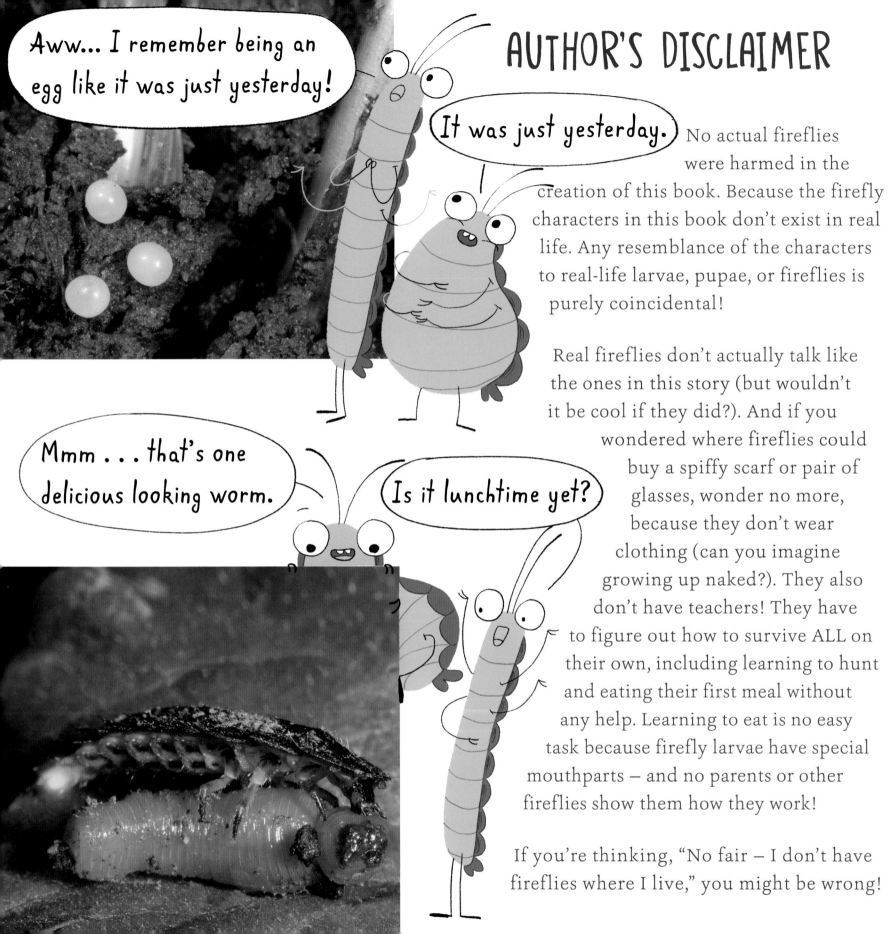

Aww... I remember being an egg like it was just yesterday!

It was just yesterday.

Mmm . . . that's one delicious looking worm.

Is it lunchtime yet?

He's blinding me with his bioluminescence!

Fireflies are nocturnal, so they are active when you're asleep in your bed, and they spend their time as larvae and pupae underground where you can't see them anyway. Because lots of species don't glow, you might not realize they are living in your backyard unless you are a super firefly detective!

We know a lot, but there is SO much more to learn! *How to Survive as a Firefly* was written based on current research and what the scientists who study them believe to be true.

Special thanks to the following experts who devoted their time to learn and share information with us about these fascinating beetles:

DON SALVATORE
Firefly Watch coordinator
Museum of Science Boston
https://legacy.mos.org/fireflywatch/

BEN PFEIFFER
Firefly researcher/founder of
Firefly.org
www.firefly.org

Play dead! Play dead!

GLOSSARY

METAMORPHOSIS: The changes that some animals go through in how they look and act during the process of becoming adults.

LIFE CYCLE: The stages of life from birth to death.

PREDATOR: An animal that eats other animals.

INSECT: A small animal with six legs and a body made of three parts (head, thorax, and abdomen). Insects may also have wings.

NOCTURNAL: A creature that is asleep during the day and awake at night.

BIOLUMINESCENCE: Light produced from living things.

AGGRESSIVE MIMICRY: When a predator changes how it looks or acts to trick you, so that it can eat you.

PHOTINUS PYRALIS: A beetle that flies and also produces light. Also known as the common eastern firefly and the big dipper firefly, it is the most common species of firefly in North America.

PHOTURIS: Another common beetle in North America, this genus also flies and produces light. Known as the femme fatale firefly, the female fireflies of this genus copy the flashing pattern of the *Photinus* females, in order to trick the *Photinus* males. When the *Photinus* male approaches the female, she will kill and eat him.